Shining Brow

Paul Muldoon was educated at Queen's University, Belfast, and then worked as a radio producer for the BBC in Northern Ireland. He now lives in America, and teaches at Princeton University.

by the same author

NEW WEATHER (1973)
MULES (1977)
WHY BROWNLEE LEFT (1980)
QUOOF (1983)
SELECTED POEMS 1968–1983 (1986)
MEETING THE BRITISH (1987)
MADOC (1990)

THE FABER BOOK OF
CONTEMPORARY IRISH POETRY (*editor*) (1986)

PAUL MULDOON

Shining Brow

faber and faber

LONDON · BOSTON

First published in 1993
by Faber and Faber Limited
3 Queen Square London WCIN 3AU

Photoset by Wilmaset Ltd, Birkenhead, Wirral
Printed in England by Clays Ltd, St Ives plc

A CIP record for this book is available from the British Library

ISBN 0–571–16789–6

This opera was commissioned by Madison Opera, a division of the
Madison Civic Music Association of Madison, Wisconsin,
where it received its première in April 1993.

I gratefully acknowledge a Fellowship from the
John Simon Guggenheim Memorial Foundation for 1990-91.
                                                      P.M.

2 4 6 8 10 9 7 5 3 1

for Daron Aric Hagen

DRAMATIS PERSONAE

FRANK LLOYD WRIGHT architect	high lyric baritone
MAMAH CHENEY one of his clients	soprano
LOUIS SULLIVAN Wright's mentor	tenor
EDWIN CHENEY Mamah's husband	bass
CATHERINE WRIGHT THIRD WOMAN *and* MAID	lyric soprano
WAITER, CHEF	spoken role
TWO CHILDREN	

MIXED CHORUS of Draftsmen, Construction Workers, Townspeople, Reporters, Photographers, Party Guests, Firemen and Taliesin Staff

Onstage Piano Trio and Dancers

PROLOGUE

Chicago, 1903. A dimly lit corner, stage right, of the Cliff Dwellers'
Club where LOUIS SULLIVAN *is slumped at a table, an empty glass*
before him. He has been drinking throughout the afternoon; his
thoughts are correspondingly muddled.

SULLIVAN

So much so, that even now I flinch
at the very thought of a stone taking wing
from Madison, Wisconsin;

it was every inch
a proud and soaring thing
that, true to form following function,

lodged itself in my brow.
As I did in his. I was his *Lieber Meister*.
He was a 'pencil in my hand'.

(*A* WAITER *enters, bearing a drink on a tray.*)

WAITER

Mr Sullivan, sir. Your brandy and *crème de menthe*.

SULLIVAN

(*Ignoring him*)

I was his *Lieber Meister*; he was a 'pencil in my hand';
together we would make our mark
on the clean slate of America.

WAITER

Kowtow, kowtow, kowtow, kowtow, kowtow.
He's already three sheets in the wind.

SULLIVAN

We dreamed of a mile-high building with a huge
                                        tap-root;
but his ambition, or my pride –
it's hard to say exactly which –
would drive a wedge
between us . . .

WAITER
Sir, your brandy and *crème de menthe*.

SULLIVAN
And this, perhaps, is how things were meant
to be; for Troy must fall, Achilles must slay Hector.

WAITER
(*Anticipating* SULLIVAN)
And therein lies . . .

SULLIVAN
And therein lies . . .

DRAFTSMEN (*off*)
And therein lies the poetry . . .

(*The* WAITER *exits.*)

SULLIVAN
And therein lies the poetry of architecture.

(SULLIVAN *drains his glass. A pool of light illuminates him
throughout the ensuing scene.*)

Orchestral segue.

ACT ONE

SCENE I

*Chicago, 1903. Lights up on Frank Lloyd Wright's bustling office.
A male* CHORUS *of twenty* DRAFTSMEN *at twenty drawing-boards,
seen from rear; each drawing-board is equipped with a work-light.*

DRAFTSMEN
The poetry of architecture
is a poetry of vision;
we set our sights
on unscaled heights
with our ground-plans and elevations.

The poetry of architecture
is a poetry of tension;
we take as our theme
the brick and the beam
and we add an extra dimension.

But the poetry of architecture
is not without its laws;
there's someone at the bottom
of every totem-
pole: you can't make bricks without straw.

The poetry of architecture
is a poetry that's rooted
in our bearing much more stress
than a flying buttress
though our fame is less often bruited.

So the poetry of architecture
is a poetry that's composed
by a chorus of slaves
much like ourselves
who get shunted from pillar to post.

For the poetry of architecture
has its Masters and its Schools;
some are destined to stand
with their pencils in their hands . . .

(WRIGHT *enters*.)

WRIGHT
And some are destined to rule.

(WRIGHT *is followed by* EDWIN *and* MAMAH CHENEY, *whom he
ushers to his desk, on which are spread the plans of various houses*.)

DRAFTSMEN
(*Sheepishly*, sotto voce)
Some are destined to stand
with their pencils in their hands
and some are destined to rule.

WRIGHT
The poetry of architecture, Mr and Mrs Cheney,
is universal. The Sioux and the Shoshone
might have taught the Greeks and Romans
a lesson in harmony.

MAMAH
I can't quite imagine the appeal to John Ruskin
of a few sticks covered with deer-skins.

EDWIN
Mamah, please.

MAMAH
In any case, we might as justly speak of
the 'music'
of architecture.

WRIGHT

Indeed we might. Be it mud hut,
                    mansion or mosque,
cabin, cathedral or kraal –
they should all be somehow integral.

DRAFTSMEN

They should all be somehow integral.

(WRIGHT *comes round to the front of the desk and stands beside*
MAMAH.)

WRIGHT

And Mah-mah – if I may?

MAMAH

(*Correcting his pronunciation*)
May-mah – if you would.

DRAFTSMEN

Mah-mah. May-mah. My, my, my.

WRIGHT

May I say that what's uppermost in my mind
when I take my pencil in my hand
to draw up a plan for *your* Utopia, *your* Erewhon,
is that form and function are one.

MAMAH

What a curious expression – 'my pencil in my hand'.

DRAFTSMEN

We know pretty much exactly what he has in mind
when he mentions his 'pencil in his hand'.

WRIGHT

Take, for example, this house in Buffalo;
each room opens into the next, so one may follow

one's bent, as it were, from the living room
through the den to the bedroom . . .

EDWIN

It's faintly reminiscent of a maze . . .

MAMAH

But a maze in which one finds oneself, my sweet,
the way the greatest rivers most meander.

EDWIN

The way in every labyrinth there lurks a Minotaur.

WRIGHT

Over the lintel of the hearth
in this house in Buffalo is carved;

> *The reality of the house is order*
> *The blessing of the house is community*
> *The glory of the house is hospitality*
> *The crown of the house is godliness*

DRAFTSMEN

> *The reality of the house is order*
> *The blessing of the house is community*
> *The glory of the house is hospitality*
> *The crown of the house is godliness*

MAMAH

What a curious sloping roof.

WRIGHT

That, Mamah, is a
hip-roof;
so called, I might say, because it follows the curve . . .

EDWIN

Far be it from me to lower the tone
of these proceedings, but when all's said and done
there's the little matter of how much it'll cost . . .

MAMAH

Edwin, you sound like Banquo's ghost.

DRAFTSMEN

It's almost six. Time to call it a day.

WRIGHT

It's still a tad early to say
exactly. I'll have a more concrete idea
by the end of the week.

MAMAH

   Oh, Eddie,
the cost is as nothing to the worth
of a house designed by Frank Lloyd Wright.

EDWIN

Just so long as it doesn't cost the earth.

(EDWIN *and* MAMAH CHENEY *take their leave.*)

MAMAH

(*Extending her hand*)
  Until the end of the week.

WRIGHT

(*Kissing her hand*)
     Until then, Mamah.

EDWIN

(*Abruptly*)
       Goodnight.

(The DRAFTSMEN *leave their drawing-boards, automaton-like, each switching off his work-light.)*

DRAFTSMEN

The music, so . . . the music of architecture
is a music that takes its tempo
from the hammer blows
and the to and fro
of the saw in the wrist and the temple.

The music of architecture
is the music that stirs the heart
with a passion so profound
as can only be found
in the highest forms of art.

The music of architecture
is a music that stems from the breast;
but there's many a slip
'twixt cup and lip:
so much gets compromised.

For the music of architecture
has a theme that's rarely stated;
the bottom line
of nickels and dimes
and cheques that are always post-dated.

The music of architecture
is the music of the human soul,
but, take it from us,
it ain't worth a cuss
without a great, big, fat bank-roll.

The trick is this; how to reconcile
these irreconcilable factors:
now that Wright's left at least one of the Cheneys
in no doubt of his genius,
he can only hope . . .

(*The last* DRAFTSMAN *is clearing his drawing-board.* WRIGHT
leans against his own desk in a warm pool of light.)

WRIGHT

Her hip . . .

DRAFTSMAN

He can only hope to make . . .

WRIGHT

I can only hope to make . . .

(*The* DRAFTSMAN *turns out his light and leaves.*)

DRAFTSMAN

To make and remake the music of architecture.

WRIGHT

And her scent. Was it musk?

(WRIGHT *is alone at his desk, his 'pencil in his hand'.*)

Not musk. Cedar perhaps. Perhaps night-scented stock.
It all goes back to those Froebel blocks
my mama gave me as a child.
La Belle Dame sans Merci, The Lady of Shalott –
these were my first patrons; I was their Master Builder.
Not stock. Saxifrage. A flower to split a boulder
in the prairie of men's hearts;

(*Unbeknownst to him,* CATHERINE WRIGHT *comes into the office.*)

she has pierced my heart like an arrowhead.

CATHERINE

Frank, my dear.

WRIGHT

Catherine. What brings you here?

9

CATHERINE

An arrowhead? But this is all so sudden.
Is it jasper or obsidian?

WRIGHT

What brings you here?

CATHERINE

Is it Minnetaree or Mandan?

WRIGHT

What brings you here?

CATHERINE

If Mahomet won't come to the mountain . . .

WRIGHT

Catherine, my dear.

CATHERINE

We've scarcely spoken in a month.

(SULLIVAN *briefly comes to, delivers line, then slumps.*)

SULLIVAN

Another brandy and *crème de menthe*.

CATHERINE

If not for mine, then for the children's sakes,
come home one evening at six
if only to play a nursery game.
I doubt if you even remember their names.
Have you forgotten those evenings in Oak Park
when we built upon the built-up dark
and climbed aboard the old toboggan
and ate roast chestnuts and pecans?
At least do me the honour . . .

WRIGHT

Lloyd Junior . . .

CATHERINE

. . . of considering whether you'll join . . .

WRIGHT

John . . .

CATHERINE

. . . me for a late dinner.

WRIGHT

Kate Junior . . .

CATHERINE

I'll wear the taffeta . . .

WRIGHT

David . . .

CATHERINE

. . . dress and the pendant that reads *Semper Virens* . . .

WRIGHT

Frances . . .

CATHERINE

. . . given to me by Louis Sullivan . . .

WRIGHT

Llewellyn . . .

CATHERINE

For though I may have grown a little stout . . .

WRIGHT

Has anybody been left out?

CATHERINE
. . . still and all, Frank, still and all . . .

WRIGHT
(*Insistently*)
Has anybody been left out?

CATHERINE
All of us. We've all been shut out by the wall
you've thrown up round yourself,
while your pursuit of fame and wealth
would be laughable . . .

WRIGHT
It all goes back to Froebel.

CATHERINE
. . . if it weren't so cruel.

WRIGHT
All somehow integral.

CATHERINE
A paradox, Frank. Your public espousal of the ideal
of family life – all that tittle-tattle
carved on lintels and picked out in tesserae –
while your own life's in disarray.
As for your prattle about 'integrity' . . .

WRIGHT
(*Spoken*)
I'll be home no later than nine-thirty.

(CATHERINE *begins to move towards door.*)

CATHERINE
Did I mention, by the way, that a couple of fellows
came by today with your new automobile?

WRIGHT

They did?

CATHERINE

They did indeed. They just drove it into the yard
and were sloping off when I yelled
after them.

WRIGHT

You did?

CATHERINE

I did indeed. And, you know, one of these fellows
turned on his heel
(CATHERINE *begins to move back towards him.*)
and came towards me, without saying a word,
and held out a little card.

WRIGHT

He did?

CATHERINE

He did indeed. I could have sworn it read
something like 'Mephistopheles'.

WRIGHT

A mite heavy-handed, if you'll allow.

CATHERINE

His hand, Frank, was cold.

WRIGHT

The paintwork? Is it gold?

CATHERINE

The canopy is black, my dear, but it's mostly yellow.

(CATHERINE *exits, leaving* WRIGHT *alone at his desk. At the Cliff Dwellers' Club*, SULLIVAN *comes to, opens a copy of the* Chicago Tribune, *puts his feet up and begins to read.*)

WRIGHT

Each room opens into the next, so one may follow
one's bent, as it were, from glade through sylvan
glade – till the valley of disenchantment
gives way to the Great Plains. There Louis Sullivan
and I dreamed of a mile-high building with a huge
                                                    tap-root
that was every inch a proud and soaring thing.

Only the other day I read a newspaper report
of a man who complained of an ache in his chest.
When they opened him up they found a lump
of gristle and keratin
big as a baby's fist;
that lump was his own twin
whom he'd ousted in their mother's womb.
Not stock. Not saxifrage. Gardenia.

(SULLIVAN *puts down his paper, nurses his drink.*)

He was my *Lieber Meister*; I was a 'pencil in his hand';

(WRIGHT *is now ghosted by* SULLIVAN.)

together we would make our mark
on the clean slate of America.
But my ambition, or his pride –
it's hard to say exactly which –
would drive a wedge
between us . . .

(SULLIVAN *shrugs, drains glass.*)

What a curious name . . . 'Edwin' . . .
Edwin, Edwin, Edwin . . . Brood.
She has pierced my heart
like an arrowhead;
and the Seminole, the Sioux, the Shoshone, the Sans
                                                    Arcs –
they come sweeping back across the land
to build upon the built-up dark.

(WRIGHT *dons a distinctive overcoat and flamboyant hat, puts out the light on his desk, and begins to walk out.*)

Orchestral interlude based on 'Hymn to Nature', a piece generally attributed to Goethe.

SCENE 2

Oak Park, Illinois. Six months later. The site of the Cheney house, initially in mid-construction, though the building gradually materializes during the course of the scene. The lighting suggests a progress from early morning to dusk, so the MALE CHORUS *of* WORKMEN *will eventually be silhouetted against the sky. The* CHORUS *is augmented by* DANCERS, *whose gestures are highly stylized. One by one, the* WORKMEN *enter, and begin to clamber on to the structure of the house.*

FIRST WORKMAN
When I woke up this morning, I was still in my
                                dungarees.

SECOND WORKMAN
When he woke up this morning, he was still in his
                                dungarees.

FIRST WORKMAN
I steadied myself at the washstand with a shot of
                                Tanqueray.

15

SECOND WORKMAN

Hand me up my spirit-level, my plumb-line and my
plumb.

FIRST AND THIRD WORKMEN

Hand that man his spirit-level, his plumb-line and his
plumb.

SECOND WORKMAN

Hand me up my spirit-level, or I'll lose my equilibrium.

FIRST AND THIRD WORKMEN

Your what?

SECOND WORKMAN

My *equilibrium*.

THIRD WORKMAN

When the whistle blew at lunchtime, I opened my
lunch-pail.

FIRST, SECOND AND FOURTH WORKMEN

When the whistle blew at lunchtime, we opened our
lunch-pails.

THIRD WORKMAN

Mine was completely empty . . .

ALL

That's why his mouth is full of
nails.

FOURTH WORKMAN

With our mouths full of nails, and our hammers in our
hands . . .

(*The* FOURTH WORKMAN *bangs his thumb.*)

ALL

With our mouths full of nails and our hammers in our
                                                hands . . .

FOURTH WORKMAN

We came sweeping back, back across the land.

FIFTH WORKMAN

We started out to build on the 'prairie of men's hearts'.

ALL

The what?

FIFTH WORKMAN

I said, the 'prairie of men's hearts'.

ALL

We started out to build on 'the prairie of men's hearts'.

(*The* FIRST WORKMAN *now has a vantage point high in the rafters
of the house, from where he gives a wolf whistle.*)

FIRST WORKMAN

Look out below. Here comes a bit of skirt.

ALL

We had to dig down deep till we hit something hard.

(*The* FIRST WORKMAN *gives another wolf whistle.*)

FIRST WORKMAN

Dig deep, little lady, I'll give you something hard.

ALL

We had to dig down deep till we touched the common
                                                clay.

(*One by one, the* CHORUS *of the women of Oak Park enter,
ignoring the wolf whistles and catcalls.*)

SECOND WORKMAN
These Oak Park ladies are so terribly lah-de-dah.

ALL
Then and only then would we see the light of day.

THIRD WORKMAN
We had to dig down deep till we heard the tell-tale
knock . . .

ALL
We had to dig down deep till we heard the tell-tale
knock
of Aaron's rod . . .

FOURTH AND FIFTH WORKMEN
(*Lewdly*)
. . . of Aaron's rod . . .

ALL
of Aaron's rod against the old bed-rock.

FIRST WOMAN
Far be it from me to suggest that these ruffians could
lower the tone
of the neighbourhood, since it's already been lowered
out of all recognition.

THIRD WOMAN
You mean by Frank Lloyd Wright.

FIRST WOMAN
By Frank Lloyd Wright and the Cheney woman.
It's an open secret, how they drive about in that
'Yellow Devil'.

18

FIRST WORKMAN

(*Lewdly*)

Just like Billy Glasscock. You could see him coming
a mile away.

SECOND WOMAN

Wright's the very embodiment of evil.

FIRST WOMAN

At speeds of up to fifteen miles an hour.

THIRD WOMAN

He's just another man of forty, turning his back on
years of connubial
bliss.

SECOND WOMAN

While she's no better than a common whore.

THIRD WOMAN

My heart goes out to Catherine Wright. So pure. So
noble.
So noble, yet so woebegone.
I saw her only yesterday, here in Oak Park;
she muttered something about chestnuts and roast
pecans
and building upon the built-up dark.

CHORUS OF WOMEN OF OAK PARK

It's an open secret that Wright and the Cheney woman
drive about in the 'Yellow Devil'
at speeds of up to fifteen miles an hour;

(*The* WOMEN *begin to disperse as the* WORKMEN *take up the
chorus.*)

WORKMEN

He's the very embodiment of evil,

WOMEN
while she's no better than a common whore.

FIRST WORKMAN
Look lively, lads. Back to your posts.
Here comes Ed Cheney.

(*The* WORKMEN *recollect themselves as* EDWIN CHENEY *enters;
they pointedly ignore him as he inspects the house.*)

We had to dig down deep with our picks and long-
tailed shovels.

ALL
We had to dig down deep with our picks and long-
tailed shovels.

FIRST WORKMAN
With our awls and our augers we bored and bored and
bored.

EDWIN
Three long days and three long nights in the belly of
the beast
was as much as Jonah
could bear; for more
than three months, I've been trapped in the hump-
backed whale
of this so-called 'prairie house'.

SECOND WORKMAN
My mother was a Mohawk, my father used to stay out
nights.

ALL
His mother was a Mohawk, his father used to stay out
nights.

SECOND WORKMAN
That must be why I'm blessed with such a head for
heights.

THIRD WORKMAN
I had to dig down deep, deep into my old lunch-pail.

ALL
He had to dig down deep, deep into his old lunch-pail.
It was completely empty . . .

EDWIN
(*Calling up to the* FIRST WORKMAN.)
You.

FIRST WORKMAN
Me?

EDWIN
You on the girder. Yes, *you*.

FIRST WORKMAN
This is no girder, Mr Cheney. This is a 'truss'.

EDWIN
I'm a little concerned by the roof. I mean, its *angle*.

FIRST WORKMAN
Let down your plumb-line, Jimmy.

SECOND WORKMAN
(*Sarcastically*)
Me?

FIRST WORKMAN
Yes, *you*. Let down your plumb. Let's see how it
dangles.

(*The* SECOND WORKMAN *pays out his plumb-line*.)

SECOND WORKMAN
It's straight as a die. It's perfectly true.

FIRST WORKMAN
There you have it, Mr Cheney. It's as true as . . .

EDWIN
As true as what?

FIRST WORKMAN
It's as true as . . . truth.
You have to remember that this is a hip-roof,
so called, I might say, because it follows the curve . . .

EDWIN
I know, I know, I know; I know
only too well the features of the 'prairie house' –
its walls of rain, its window-panes of ice,
its door of wind, its roof of hard-packed snow,
and, at its core, a vast emptiness.

The truth is that my mouth is full of nails.

For three long months I've hunkered in the maw,
bowed under, mortgaged to the hilt,
and pondered the universal law;
for everything that's built
something is destroyed.

(EDWIN *spots a flint on the ground, picks it up*.)

So it was that the Master Builder
assigned Prometheus his rock
and Sisyphus his boulder

(EDWIN *scrutinizes the flint*.)

and Job his little pot-sherd;
I do believe it's an arrowhead.

(EDWIN *puts the flint in his breast-pocket, then stands in the door-frame, extending both arms.*)

For three long months I myself have been the grist
to Frank Lloyd Wright's grist-mill.
I've been stretched upon the rack.
I've put my shoulder
to the burning wheel.
More than once I've been pinned up by my wings.
  Instead of the cross, the Albatross
  about my neck is hung.
Everything's out of kilter.
The very house stands at a list;
there's not a line that's not somehow askew.

(EDWIN CHENEY *retreats within the house.*)

SECOND WORKMAN
(*Reeling it in*)
They say the soul weighs about the same as a plumb-
                                            line and a plumb.

ALL
There are souls that weigh far more than a plumb-line
                                            and a plumb.

FOURTH WORKMAN
(*Examining it*)
There's a blood blister on my thumb.

ALL
With one eye on our plumb-lines, one on our spirit-
                                            levels,
it's as much as most of us can do to keep our
                                            equilibrium.

23

FIRST WORKMAN
Look out below, here comes the 'Yellow Devil'.

(*The lights go down even further on the* WORKMEN.)

FIFTH WORKMAN
I'd sawn halfway through a plank. Now I can't see my
mark.

ALL
He'd sawn halfway through a plank. Now he's lost his
mark.

FIFTH WORKMAN
It's the fate of every carpenter to fade into his own
woodwork.

(WRIGHT *and* MAMAH CHENEY *draw up in an extravagant yellow
automobile. They are in buoyant spirits, oblivious of* EDWIN, *or the*
WORKMEN, *who continue* sotto voce.)

ALL
We know, we know, we know; we know
only too well the features of the 'prairie house' –
its walls of rain, its window-panes of ice,
its door of wind, its roof of hard-packed snow,
and, at its core, a vast emptiness.

(WRIGHT, *in his distinctive hat and overcoat, helps* MAMAH *out of
the automobile. Together they survey the work in progress.*)

WRIGHT
Each room opens into the next, if you remember,
like the chambers
of the heart.

WORKMEN

(Sotto voce)
> And, at its core, a vast emptiness.

(WRIGHT *goes down on one knee.*)

WRIGHT

(*Spoken*)
> *As the kiss of two lovers at night*
> *Makes the darkness a choir,*
> *The dusk is a-quiver with light*
> *Of its heart's desire.*

MAMAH

(*Extending her hand*)
> Oh, Frank, you've such a way with words.

WRIGHT

(*Taking her hand*)
> Those were the words of the Welsh bard,
> Taliesin,
> to the Lady of the Lake,
> with whom he . . .

MAMAH

> had a secret liaison?

WRIGHT

> Something of that ilk.

MAMAH

> A lovers' tryst?

WRIGHT

> She was less a lover than a muse.

MAMAH

> How dull. So it's what you might call an allusion?

WRIGHT

I borrowed those lines from a masque
by a certain Richard Hovey.

MAMAH

Do you mean 'borrowed' or 'purloined'?

WRIGHT

Borrowed.

MAMAH

How positively dull.
(*Distractedly*)
Was the house always meant to list?
It seems somewhat topsy-turvy.

WRIGHT

Be it mud hut, mansion or mosque
a Minnetaree
earth-lodge, a cabin with the antlers of an elk
gracing its eaves –
be it the Chapel of the Holy Grail –
they should all be somehow integral.

MAMAH

It's faintly reminiscent of a maze.

WRIGHT

To borrow a phrase from my old mentor,
Louis Sullivan . . .

(EDWIN CHENEY *sings out from within the house.*)

EDWIN

In every labyrinth . . .

26

(WRIGHT *starts, releases* MAMAH's *hand and gets to his feet as* EDWIN *appears in the doorway.*)

there lurks . . .

MAMAH

Eddie . . .

WRIGHT

a Minotaur.

MAMAH

You sound like Banquo's ghost.

EDWIN

Far be it from me to lower the tone
of these proceedings, but when all's said and done
there's the little matter of the Wedding Guest.

MAMAH

Please, Eddie. Try not to be distraught.

EDWIN

I've just been pondering the motto over the hearth.
I think it should read;
  *For everything that's built
  something is destroyed.*

WRIGHT

I hope you don't mind, Ed; I borrowed your wife
for the afternoon.

EDWIN

Mind? Why should I mind?
You've already cost me the earth.

MAMAH

Why so crestfallen, so forlorn?

(EDWIN *moves towards* MAMAH.)

EDWIN

So crestfallen?

(EDWIN *takes* MAMAH's *hands and presses them to his head*.)

So forlorn?

WRIGHT

In the phrase I borrowed from Louis Sullivan . . .

EDWIN

Can't you feel those little nodes
of gristle and keratin?

MAMAH

I feel nothing, Eddie.

EDWIN

For three months I've been growing horns.

(MAMAH *snatches away her hands*.)

MAMAH

You know I simply can't abide
your self-pity.

(EDWIN *puts his hands to his head*.)

EDWIN

For three long months I've sought to ease
the pain of these nodes
of gristle and keratin
but have found no salve,

28

no Balm of Gilead.
It's been to no avail,
to absolutely no avail.

MAMAH

I feel nothing, Eddie, not the merest hint
of remorse; I must follow my bent,
as it were, towards my own enfranchisement.

EDWIN

If not for mine, then for the children's sakes,
come home one evening at six;
you've made us all a laughing-stock.

MAMAH

For three long months I've been ostracized
but the nods
and winks and twitching curtains
have only strengthened my resolve;
my love for Frank Lloyd
Wright will prevail
when all else fails.

(MAMAH *moves towards* WRIGHT.)

WRIGHT

For three long months I've tried to loose
the knot,
the inextricable, Gordian
knot that binds Mamah and myself.
I'm consumed by guilt,
yet adamant as Percival
in the Chapel of the Holy Grail.

TRIO

EDWIN: ⎰ For three long months I've tried to ease
MAMAH: ⎱ For three long months I've been ostracized
WRIGHT: For three long months I've tried to loose

EDWIN:		the pain of these nodes
MAMAH:	{	but the nods
WRIGHT:		the knot,

EDWIN:		of gristle and keratin
MAMAH:	{	and winks and twitching curtains
WRIGHT:		the inextricable, Gordian

EDWIN:		but have found no salve,
MAMAH:	{	have only strengthened my resolve;
WRIGHT:		knot that binds Mamah and myself.

EDWIN:		no Balm of Gilead.
MAMAH:	{	my love for Frank Lloyd
WRIGHT:		I'm consumed by guilt,

EDWIN:		It's been to no avail,
MAMAH:	{	Wright will prevail
WRIGHT:		yet adamant as Percival

EDWIN:		to absolutely no avail.
MAMAH:	{	when all else fails.
WRIGHT:		in the Chapel of the Holy Grail.

(EDWIN *moves towards the house and stands in the door-frame.*)

WRIGHT

Each room opens into the next, like the chambers . . .

MAMAH

Please, Frank. Please don't fan the embers.

EDWIN

In the belly of the beast
there's a lump of amber-
gris.

(EDWIN *extends his arms.*)

One of these days I'll boast
a set of antlers fit to grace
the eaves of any 'prairie house'.

If all else fails,
I'll swallow hydrochloric
acid; I'd hang myself by a rope
from a purlin
if I thought it might be to some avail.

MAMAH

To absolutely no avail.
I won't go back to needlework,
to the drab
monotony of plain one, purl one.
My love for Frank Lloyd Wright will prevail.

(EDWIN *steps back into the shadows, while* WRIGHT *steers* MAMAH
towards the automobile.)

WRIGHT

Let us set sail;
together we will make our mark
on the well-worn slate of Europe;
in Rome, or Paris, or Berlin,
we'll build our Chapel of the Holy Grail.

(WRIGHT *sweeps* MAMAH *off her feet and on to the running-board
of the 'Yellow Devil'. Curtain.*)

Choral interlude based on Goethe's 'Hymn to Nature'.

CHORUS

She sweeps us off our feet
and dances round and round,
then flings us back, exhausted,
on the muddy ground.

We lie on the muddy ground
and take her in our arms.
She's nowhere to be found
amongst her thousand forms.

Though she takes a thousand forms
she's always in one place.
She takes us in her arms.
She holds us in a fast embrace.

She holds us in a fast embrace.
What seemed like flesh and blood
has vanished without trace.
Hither and thither we're pulled.

Hither and thither we're pulled
and yet we haven't strayed.
For everything that's built
something is destroyed.

That something is destroyed
is itself a grand illusion.
For everything that's destroyed
something else is built.

The door is shut. We draw the bolt.
We mount the winding stair.
With every step, we melt
back into earth and air.

Earth and air and fire and water;
all somehow integral.
We are all of us in Nature;
she is within us all.

SCENE 3

Berlin, 1910. The lights come up slowly on the drawing room of
MAMAH CHENEY's *apartment, stage left, where she sits alone, at*
work on a translation of the 'Hymn to Nature'.

MAMAH
Die Menschen sind alle in ihr und sie in allen.

(Revising her translation)

> We – are – all – within – Nature;
> she – is – within – us – all.

(MAMAH *gets up from her desk and moves towards the window.*)

> How much longer must I endure
>
> our being apart? I look out from the walls
> of Troy, like Helen
> sighing for a sail.
>
> I see nothing. Only a camisole on a clothes line
> over Friedrichstrasse.
> It might be a Rhine
>
> maiden, a damsel in distress.
> She calls to me, 'Cuckoo . . . cuckold . . . '
> as seamstress calls to seamstress
>
> across a mile-wide quilt.
> I feel nothing. Not the merest hint
> of remorse. Not a pang of guilt
>
> for having followed my bent,
> as it were, from Boone, Iowa,
> and the monotony of needlepoint
>
> to the realm of Julia Ward Howe;
> as they say in Boone –
> or used to say – *per ardua*
>
> *ad astra*. Though I went to such great pains
> to throw off my manacles of yarn . . .

(MAMAH *makes a show of wringing her hands, moves back towards the desk.*)

> the truth is that my mouth is full of pins.

(MAMAH *picks up the piece of paper*.)

>Am I destined merely to darn
>the socks of Johann Wolfgang von Goethe?

(MAMAH *sets it back on the desk and moves towards a chair*.)

>*For everything that's built*
>*something is destroyed*.

(MAMAH *runs her hand along the lapel of Wright's distinctive*
overcoat, which is draped over the chair.)

>Am I destined for ever to mend the torn
>
>pocket of Frank Lloyd Wright's top-coat?
>To be yet another vassal?
>Am I destined for ever to kowtow?
>
>To be some well-wrought urn, some pot of basil,
>into which a great man may flow?

(MAMAH *moves back towards the window*.)

>For three long months he's languished in Fiesole
>
>labouring over a portfolio
>of drawings; I sit, meanwhile, my pencil in my hand,
>and look back down the valley
>
>of disenchantment
>that runs from here to Chicago.

(SULLIVAN *sings out from the darkness, stage right*.)

SULLIVAN
Another brandy and *crème de menthe*.

34

(The lights come up gradually to reveal SULLIVAN *in his usual haunt, the Cliff Dwellers' Club. Again, he is immersed in the* Chicago Tribune.)

MAMAH

Even now I hear an echo
in the built-up dark, as Catherine, dear Catherine,
cries 'cuckold . . . cuckoo . . .'

to the Gaderene
swine in the Cliff Dwellers'
Club. While I embroider the quatrains

of Goethe's high-and-mighty verse
I hear a higher, mightier voice resound;
(She mimics CATHERINE:)
'There can be, and there will be, no divorce.'

Though he's a stag dragged down by his own hounds,
Actaeon to my Artemis,
Edwin's honour knows no bounds.

How can I redeem
myself? On a November
evening in Berlin, as the light further dims,

I look out from my chamber
at that camisole, those three sheets in the wind,
at what remains of my empire.

And perhaps I do feel the merest hint
of remorse as a violin
rehearses from the apartment

opposite the high-flown
maunderings of a new masterwork
by Richard Strauss. So much for Avalon.

So much for our making our mark
on the well-worn slate
of Europe.

35

(SULLIVAN *looks up suddenly from his newspaper*.)

SULLIVAN

An *elephant* portfolio . . .?
An elephant's graveyard, more like.

(SULLIVAN *begins to tear out a column from his newspaper, which he folds meticulously*.)

MAMAH

Only the other week

the Emperors trailed their ermine and ocelot
through Potsdam, and jostled their kindergarten
blocks. So much for Tristan and Isolde.

There's a lump of gristle and keratin
in my entrails;
for Frank has thrown up a cordon

round the Chapel of the Holy Grail,
while his pursuit of wealth and fame
would be laughable if it weren't so cruel.

(MAMAH *goes back to her desk and picks up the piece of paper*.)

Yet he is everywhere in me, and I in him.

SULLIVAN

(*Angrily*)
Another brandy, you son of a bitch.

(MAMAH *begins to fold the paper. She moves back to the chair, looking towards* SULLIVAN.)

MAMAH

We are joined, like Siamese

twins, at the hip, so it's hard to say exactly which
is which. Though his ambition, or my pride,
may drive a wedge

between us . . .

SULLIVAN
Though his ambition, or my pride,
would drive a wedge
between us . . .

MAMAH
our love is anchored by a great tap-root,
a chain that won't be broken.

(SULLIVAN *puts the folded newspaper article in his inside pocket.*
MAMAH *mirrors his action by placing the Goethe translation in the*
pocket of Wright's overcoat.)

He'll imagine some wood-nymph or water-sprite
has left this as a token

(MAMAH *lovingly 'embraces' the coat.*)

of the seeming randomness of things, the haphazard,
hidden order in a lichen

on a stone. Yet when I clasp him to my breast
I feel nothing. My hand is cold.

(MAMAH *drapes the coat over the chair and moves back towards the*
window.)

If only he were in hot pursuit

of something other than the accolades,
the bay leaves heaped on his brow.
There is no Balm in Gilead.

So much for the realm of Julia Ward Howe
and her spirit trilling like a meadow lark;
she's dead and gone. And now

the Vandals and Huns, the Goths under Alaric,
come sweeping back across the land
to build upon the built-up dark.

For though I've tried to make my stand
with all the force that I can muster,
I'm destined to be a mere 'pencil in his hand'

and he to be my *Lieber Meister*.

SULLIVAN
I was his *Lieber Meister*.

MAMAH
I stand on the edge of an abyss. I look into a chasm.

SULLIVAN
He was a 'pencil in my hand'.

MAMAH
There is no Balm in Gilead, no holy chrism
nor extreme unction
with which to anoint my shining brow. Only a
                                       cataclysm

of burning oil . . .

SULLIVAN
                  . . . form following function . . .

MAMAH
and molten lead, an avalanche
of fire and brimstone, broken glass and bricks
taking wing . . .

SULLIVAN
He was every inch
a proud and soaring thing.

MAMAH AND SULLIVAN
So much so . . .

SULLIVAN
(*Spoken*)
Bring me that brandy, you little prick.

MAMAH
So much so, that even now I flinch.

(SULLIVAN *puts his hands to his head.* MAMAH *draws the curtains in a decisive gesture. Curtain.*)

ACT TWO

SCENE I

Christmas Morning, 1911. Taliesin, Spring Green, Wisconsin. A MIXED CHORUS *of* REPORTERS, PHOTOGRAPHERS *and* TOWNSPEOPLE *of Spring Green are assembled in the living room for a long-awaited press conference. A grand piano is festooned with Christmas cards. There's a Christmas tree trimmed with ornaments; a fire blazes in the hearth.*

REPORTERS

So much, so much, so much, so much so
that even now we flinch
at the thought of all this hullabaloo
for the sake of a column inch.

For the sake of a column inch
that might nail him to the door,
how long must we endure
this following every hunch?

How long must we endure
this tally-ho and view-halloo
through spring and summer, fall and winter,
till Frank Lloyd Wright's laid low?

We've hunted high and low,
uphill and down-dale,
through wind and rain and snow;
we've never lost his trail.

We've often lost his trail
in snow or silt or sand.
Will he once again turn tail?
Or will he make a stand?

Will he once more make a stand?
Will he beat a hasty retreat?

Will he lead us a merry dance?
Will he sweep us off our feet?

He's swept us off our feet
and danced us round and round,
then flung us back, exhausted,
on the muddy ground.

We've lain on the muddy ground
like hounds shrugged off by a stag
that broke free with one bound
to stand on some rocky crag.

Once he stood on a rocky crag
and lorded it over the valley
of disenchantment. We lagged
behind. He dared us to follow.

We followed every lead,
every line of inquiry.
Not even the reek of aniseed
would divert us from our quarry.

Yet he's thrown us off the scent
and vanished without trace.
Across two continents
the door was shut in our face.

The door is shut. We draw the bolt.
We mount the winding stair.
As the otter has his holt
so the wolf must have his lair.

As the wolf becomes his lair
so the hare becomes his form.
He melts into thin air.
He takes a thousand forms.

Though he takes a thousand forms
the fox must have a den.
He must one day run to earth.
He must one day go to ground.

We've kept an ear to the ground
for every tell-tale sign.
We've finally tracked him down
to his fastness in Taliesin.

With a tally-ho and a view-halloo
we've tracked him to Spring Green.

FIRST REPORTER
When will he stop all this ballyhoo?

SECOND REPORTER
When will he ever come clean?

REPORTERS
Will the old fox show us a clean
pair of heels, as has so oft been his wont,
or is *The Monarch of the Glen*
at last *The Stag at Bay*?

THIRD REPORTER
Just my luck to end
up here, on this of all days.

REPORTERS
On this, of all days,
when the King of the World was born,
we've hot-footed it all the way
out to this . . . to this . . .

FIRST TOWNSWOMAN
(*Snidely*)

This *barn*.

REPORTERS
To Frank Lloyd Wright, this 'barn'
is a 'house that hill might marry'.

(*A disgruntled* FIRST PHOTOGRAPHER *comes over to the* FIRST
REPORTER *for some clarification.*)

FIRST PHOTOGRAPHER
A house that what?

FIRST REPORTER
(*Making it clear*)
'A – house – that – hill – might – marry.'

FIRST TOWNSWOMAN
It's my belief that Sodom and Gomorrah
wouldn't hold a candle
to Spring Green.

FIRST PHOTOGRAPHER
How will I know which one is Wright?

SECOND TOWNSWOMAN
Well said, Myra.

FIRST REPORTER
Just point your camera
at anything that moves.

FIRST TOWNSWOMAN
Not when it comes to good, old-fashioned scandal.
And, you know, Mavis . . .

FIRST PHOTOGRAPHER
Come on, Bud. I need a better handle.

TOWNSPEOPLE
Scandal. Scandal. Sodom and Gomorrah
wouldn't hold a candle
to the flesh-pots of Spring Green.

FIRST TOWNSWOMAN
Not all the frankincense and myrrh
borne by the three wise kings
would rid us of the stink
of that billy-goat
and his minx . . .

SECOND TOWNSWOMAN
. . . his shrew . . .

FIRST TOWNSWOMAN
. . . his vixen.

FIRST PHOTOGRAPHER
How will I know which one is Wright?
You'll have to give me a clue.

FIRST TOWNSWOMAN
I believe I'll die of asphyxiation.

FIRST REPORTER
He'll be wearing the same kind of hat and coat
as the fellow on a packet of Quaker Oats.

SECOND TOWNSWOMAN
Not since Sodom and Gomorrah
has anyone launched such an assault
on everything we hold dear.

FIRST PHOTOGRAPHER
And Mamah Cheney? How will I recognize her?

FIRST REPORTER
Keep your eyes peeled for a pillar of salt.

TOWNSPEOPLE
No one has launched such a fierce assault
on everything we hold dear,
not since the days of Sodom and . . .

(WRIGHT *and* MAMAH CHENEY *enter.* MAMAH *keeps a discreet distance while* WRIGHT, *in his distinctive hat and coat, greets the assembly.*)

WRIGHT

Good morrow.

TOWNSPEOPLE
Gomorrah.

WRIGHT
Good morrow.

REPORTERS AND PHOTOGRAPHERS
Gomorrah. Gomorrah. Gomorrah.

(WRIGHT *adopts a strategic position by the hearth, with* MAMAH *behind him, slightly to one side.* WRIGHT's *public pronouncements are intercut with private ruminations.*)

WRIGHT
(*Public*)
Ladies and gentlemen, let me take this occasion
to welcome you to Taliesin.

(WRIGHT *reaches into his pocket to retrieve his prepared statement, from which he reads.*)

(*Public*)
For seven long years I have withstood
the slings and arrows
of the fourth estate.
I am a man of sorrow

and acquainted with grief.
It's fitting that, today of all days,
I should most humbly crave
your indulgence. Let me say my say.

You know only too well
the details of my private life,
how a great misfortune befell
myself and my wife,

how we drifted further and further
apart.
Can a man be a faithful husband and father
and devote himself to his art?

(*Private*)

    The truth is that I never
    gave Catherine her proper due.
    I have been a traitor
    to my wife, my friends, to architecture.

(*Public*)

    I was forced to choose. The choice
    I made
    gives me no cause to rejoice.
    My mouth is full of brine.

(*Private*)

    The truth is that I feel
    nothing, not the merest hint
    of remorse.
    Not a pang of guilt.

(*Public*)

    You know only too well
    what happened next. I was enthralled
    by this blessed damozel.

(WRIGHT *gestures towards* MAMAH.)

She pierced my heart like an arrowhead.

(*Private*)
The truth is that I have been cruel.
There is a hardness in my heart.
I have torn down
many beautiful things.

The truth is that I am by nature cast
in the role of the iconoclast.
I have torn down
much that was beautiful.

The truth is that I have been cruel.
The truth is that I myself
am the hump-backed whale.
My mouth is full of krill.

Can a man be a faithful husband and father
and devote himself to his art?
The truth is that my back is to the wall.

(*Public*)
Our love is seen as a serious upheaval
of 'conventional' mores.
I'm 'the very embodiment of evil',
she's 'no better than a common whore'.

So much for the 'conventional'. The average
man may live by average laws;
the artist, however, must forge
in his own maw

some new vision of order,
an even more exacting moral code.
The artist must take a harder
and higher road,

through the dark night
of the soul towards a necessary light.

(*Private*)

The truth is that my back is to the wall.
The truth, the truth . . .

(*Public*)

That necessary light comes from within;
from there, and there alone.
For seven long years we have been prey
to rumours and allegations.

I prithee now; *Let him who is without sin
cast the first stone.*
Let it lodge in the 'Shining Brow'
of Taliesin.

For, just as Taliesin is not 'on', but 'of',
a gently sloping hill,
so my love
for Mamah Cheney is truly integral.

This is our Avalon.
This is our Chapel of the Holy Grail.

(WRIGHT *begins to fold his prepared speech.*)

(*Public*)

Now, ladies and gentlemen, we wish you all
a very merry
Christmas. We hope you will
join us in a glass of sherry,
here in this house that hill
might marry.

(*There follows a flurry of spoken questions from the agitated*
REPORTERS *and* TOWNSPEOPLE.)

FIRST REPORTER

Never mind a 'house that hill might marry';
when are you gonna marry Mamah Cheney?

FIRST TOWNSWOMAN

Did you have to find Avalon in Wisconsin?

FIRST PHOTOGRAPHER

Could I see a bit more of your chin?

SECOND TOWNSWOMAN

Don't you have any qualms of conscience?

FIRST REPORTER

Who?

FIRST TOWNSWOMAN

How?

FIRST PHOTOGRAPHER

What?

SECOND TOWNSWOMAN

Where?

FIRST REPORTER

When?

THIRD REPORTER

Why should Frank Lloyd Wright be above and beyond
the 'average' laws for 'average' men?

WRIGHT

(*Impatiently*)

    The artist must take a harder
    and higher road.
    And that, ladies and gentlemen,
    is my final word.

(WRIGHT *ushers* MAMAH *over towards the Christmas tree. They sing a descant above the* CHORUS *of* TOWNSPEOPLE, REPORTERS *and* PHOTOGRAPHERS, *who gradually begin to disperse, though the* FIRST PHOTOGRAPHER *and the* FIRST, SECOND *and* THIRD REPORTERS *drift upstage.*)

CHORUS

He's swept us off our feet
and danced us round and round
then flung us back, exhausted,
on the muddy ground.

WRIGHT

Together, Mamah, we will take that harder
and higher road.
You pierced my heart like an arrowhead.
You did me mortal hurt.

MAMAH

(*Teasing him*)

An arrowhead? But this is all so sudden.
It is jasper or obsidian?

WRIGHT

Mamah, please, try to maintain . . .

MAMAH

Is it Minnetaree or Mandan?

CHORUS

So much so
that even now we flinch
at the thought of all this hullabaloo
for the sake of a column inch.

MAMAH

Can a man devote himself to his art
and be a faithful husband and father?

WRIGHT

A great man may be true to both.
He need never choose
one path
over another.
You, Mamah, are both mother
and muse.
When all is said and done
you are both key- and corner-stone.

MAMAH

Did I mention, by the way . . . ?

WRIGHT

Not the automobile?

MAMAH

No. Did I mention that Mabel . . . ?

WRIGHT

Mabel? Who's Mabel?

MAMAH

The new maid. Remember? From Oak Park.

WRIGHT

Mabel? Of course. Mabel from Oak Park.
Could her bite be any worse than her bark?

MAMAH

Please, Frank. Don't be contrary.

WRIGHT

I'm not contrary.

(WRIGHT *picks an ornament from the crib under the tree*.)

Is this a camel or a dromedary?

MAMAH

It's just that Mabel has taken the day off.

WRIGHT

Today, of all days, to have taken off?

MAMAH

And left everything to Carleton.

WRIGHT

She's faintly reminiscent of my wife.

MAMAH

You remember Julian Carleton? The chef?

(*The* CHORUS *has now exited, except for the* FIRST
PHOTOGRAPHER *and the* FIRST, SECOND *and* THIRD
REPORTERS, *who will form an impromptu quartet.*)

THIRD REPORTER

Just my luck to end
up here . . .

SECOND REPORTER

. . . on this, of all days . . .

(*The* FIRST REPORTER *reaches into his hip-pocket.*)

FIRST REPORTER

I've got something here to revive
your spirits and warm the cockles of your hearts.

FIRST PHOTOGRAPHER

I still don't know which one is Wright.

FIRST REPORTER

This, gentlemen, is a hip-flask;
so called, I might say, because it follows the curve . . .

52

(*The* FIRST REPORTER *hands the hip-flask to the* SECOND; *all four take a swig.*)

MAMAH

Which means, Frank, I may have to ask
you to carve
the goose
when we all sit down to lunch.

SECOND REPORTER

What is this stuff? It packs a powerful punch.

WRIGHT

By all means, my dear. But don't they have geese
in Barbados
or wherever it is Carleton purports
to be from?

FIRST REPORTER

It's Demerara rum.

MAMAH

If not, I'm sure he learned to lop
the legs and wings
from any number of dead or dying things
where he last hung out his shingle.

THIRD REPORTER

My tonsils are all a-tingle.

WRIGHT

Where did he last hang out his shingle?

MAMAH

Have you forgotten? The Cliff Dwellers' Club.

WRIGHT

How many are we, in any case?

MAMAH

Have you forgotten?

FIRST REPORTER

It all comes down to the question . . .

WRIGHT

William Weston . . .

SECOND REPORTER

Of how we should act in the best . . .

WRIGHT

His son, Ernest . . .

THIRD REPORTER

Interests of our readers. Should we fan the flames . . .

WRIGHT

David Lindblom . . .

FIRST REPORTER

Of their outrage and anger . . .

WRIGHT

Thomas Brunker . . .

SECOND REPORTER

And consign Wright to the lowest depths of hell . . .

WRIGHT

Emil Brodelle . . .

THIRD REPORTER

Or should we leave him be to flout . . .

WRIGHT

Has anybody been left out?

54

The 'average' laws of 'average' men?

MAMAH
No one, Frank. We're all shut in
by the wall
you've thrown up round yourself.

FIRST PHOTOGRAPHER
I, for one, could get very, very . . .

WRIGHT
(*Again examining the ornament*)
Is this a camel or a dromedary?

FIRST PHOTOGRAPHER
Tired of this tally-ho and view-halloo
and all the news that's fit to print
on some two-bit architect and his bint.

MAMAH
A dromedary's black, my dear; a camel's mostly yellow.

(*The lights go down on* WRIGHT *and* MAMAH, *who exit, leaving the
quartet upstage.*)

FIRST PHOTOGRAPHER
I, for one, would prefer to know
how Amundsen's faring in the ice and snow.

Interlude

QUARTET
When all's said and done we'd like to know
if Amundsen has reached the Pole.
Has he been struck some cruel blow?
Is he eaten by a whale?

Has he stumbled through a hole?
Is he lying at the bottom of the sea?
Going down,
going down,
going down in history.

At the end of the day we'd like to hear
some word of the anarchist plot
to kill the Emperor
of Japan. How goes it with the suffragettes?
Why was Canalejas shot?
Is China still our cup of tea?
Going down,
going down,
going down in history.

Nineteen twelve. The Greeks and Turks
fight a familiar duel.
The Piltdown Men of Planter stock
scuttle Irish Home Rule.
The *Titanic* founders on a berg.
The passengers cry wee-wee-wee.
Going down,
going down,
going down in history.

Nineteen thirteen. By now Niels Bohr
has cracked the atom's nut.
The Mexican Prime Minister
and the King of Greece are shot.
New leaders roll off the conveyor
belt like Henry Ford's first Model 'T's;
going down,
going down,
going down in history.

Nineteen fourteen. The latest news
has Woodrow Wilson's
warships pounding Veracruz.
All going down. All going down.

Though it's been five years since he fell off a mule
at the San Carlos agency,
Geronimo's still going down,
going down,
going down in history.

June twenty-eighth. As the guests arrive
for a soirée at Taliesin,
a shot rings out in Sarajevo.

(*The* MAID *sings out from the darkness.*)

MAID

Canapé?

SCENE 2

*28 June 1914. The lights come up quickly on the living room in
Taliesin, now set for a formal party. An onstage* PIANO TRIO *plays
variations on a theme from* Der Rosenkavalier *as the* DANCERS
glide about the room.

QUARTET

June twenty-eighth. As the guests arrive
for a soirée at Taliesin,
a shot rings out in Sarajevo.
Little do they think of the repercussions
as Archduke Franz Ferdinand,
Crown Prince of Austria,
goes down,
goes down,
goes down in history.

(*The* QUARTET *exits as* WRIGHT, MAMAH *and two of her*
CHILDREN *enter. The* DANCERS *are at the heart of this scene; they
continue to glide about the room, while other* GUESTS *are ranged on
the periphery. The* MAID's *frenetic 'Canapé' points up a series of*

tableaux during which the PIANO TRIO *drops out and the action freezes.)*

MAID
(Offering a tray to WRIGHT *and* MAMAH)
Canapé?

WRIGHT
> As the kiss of two lovers at night
> Makes the darkness a choir,
> The dusk is a-quiver with light
> Of its heart's desire.

*(*WRIGHT *has gone down on one knee to present* MAMAH *with a single rose.)*

MAMAH
Those lines you borrowed from a masque
by Richard Hovey.

WRIGHT
This rose I borrowed from *Der Rosenkavalier.*

MAMAH
Ist wie ein Gruss vom Himmel.

WRIGHT
And its scent? Is it musk?

MAMAH
*Ist bereits zu stark,
als dass man's ertragen kann.*

WRIGHT
Accept it, Mamah, as a token of my love.

MAMAH

It reminds me of that night in Dresden
when we ate roast chestnuts and pecans
and built upon the built-up dark.

WRIGHT

That was the night we met Richard Strauss.

MAMAH

That was the night *you* met Richard Strauss;
I was merely a codicil
to your iron will.

WRIGHT

Accept it, Mamah, as a token of my love.

CHORUS

Is she destined to go down in history
as a codicil
to Wright's iron will?

(*The action resumes as the* MAID *makes her way among the guests.
She offers the tray to a* FIRST DRAFTSMAN *and his* WIFE.)

MAID

Canapé?

FIRST DRAFTSMAN

It's such an honour to work for Frank Lloyd Wright.

WIFE

(*Taking a canapé.*)
Even if you do sit up half the night?

FIRST DRAFTSMAN

Even if I do sit up half the night
poring over the details of Midway Gardens

I know my work will stand the test
of time.

Your work? Your work will no more stand the test
of time than this piece of toast.

(*The* WIFE *pops the canapé in her mouth.*)

FIRST DRAFTSMAN
You mean, 'crouton'.

CHORUS
Will his work no more stand the test
of time than that piece of toast,
that 'crouton'?

(*The action resumes as the* MAID *continues her progress among the
guests. She offers the tray to a* FIRST GUEST *and his* WIFE.)

MAID
Canapé?

FIRST GUEST
Is she still married to Ed Cheney?

WIFE
The Cheneys are long since divorced –
is this swordfish or tuna? –
though Wright's still married to Catherine.

MAID
Canapé?

WIFE
Is this shrimp or prawn?

FIRST GUEST

My heart goes out to Catherine Wright. So pure. So
                                                    noble.
So noble yet so woebegone.

MAID

Canapé?

WIFE

(*Taking a canapé*)
Perhaps I'll have just a little nibble.

FIRST GUEST

I saw her only the other day.
She was lunching at the Cliff Dwellers' Club
with Louis Sullivan.

(*The* CHEF *enters and approaches* WRIGHT *and* MAMAH.)

It seems that he and Frank Lloyd Wright
may shortly be reconciled.

WIFE

My mouth is full of silt.

CHORUS

Could it be that Sullivan and Wright
will shortly be reconciled?
Or will their mouths be full of silt?

(*The action resumes. The* MAID *makes her way towards* WRIGHT,
MAMAH *and the* CHEF, *who stands behind them, just within
earshot.*)

MAID

Canapé?

WRIGHT

The Chippewa, the Choctaw, the Cherokee, the
                                    Cheyenne
could have taught Cicero and Cato
a lesson in oratory.

MAMAH

Am I destined for ever to kowtow
to someone who's full of such moonshine?

CHEF

Ma'am.

MAMAH

Please don't call me by my first name.

CHEF

I said 'ma'am', ma'am.

MAMAH

Yes, Carleton.

CHEF

Might everything be in order, ma'am?

MAMAH

Everything's in order. Can it be
that all the natives of Barbados
speak with an Irish brogue?

CHEF

Whatever you say, ma'am.

CHORUS

Mamah. Mamah. Ma'am, ma'am, ma'am.
Is he destined for ever to kowtow
to someone who's full of such moonshine?

(*The action resumes. The* MAID *makes her progress among the*
GUESTS, *offering her tray to a* SECOND DRAFTSMAN *and his*
WIFE.)

MAID

Canapé?

SECOND DRAFTSMAN

It's so demeaning to work for Frank Lloyd Wright.

WIFE

(*Taking a canapé*)
At least you don't have to come home at night.

SECOND DRAFTSMAN

I'd much sooner come home at night
than pore over the details of Goethe Street.

WIFE

I find him somewhat fetching. The goatee and the strut.

(*The* WIFE *pops a canapé in her mouth.*)

SECOND DRAFTSMAN

Your mouth is full of puff pastry.
Am I destined for ever to do crewelwork
on Frank Lloyd Wright's tapestries?

CHORUS

Her mouth is full of puff pastry.
Is he destined for ever to do crewelwork
on Frank Lloyd Wright's tapestries?

(*The action resumes. The* MAID *finds her way through the throng to*
a SECOND GUEST *and his* WIFE.)

MAID

Canapé?

63

SECOND GUEST
This business of Wright and Mamah Cheney –

WIFE
They seem the very picture of connubial
bliss.

SECOND GUEST
Is as nothing compared to recent events
in China,
or Nepal,
or Austria . . .

MAID
Canapé?

WIFE
(*Taking a canapé*)
Smoked oysters?

SECOND GUEST
Morocco or Montenegro;
all pales to insignificance.

WIFE
My mouth is full of nacre.

CHEF
Why should I kowtow
to someone who calls me a cannibal,
to someone who calls me a nigger?

(*The action resumes. The* MAID *makes her way back towards*
WRIGHT, MAMAH *and the* CHEF.)

MAID
Canapé?

MAMAH

My heart goes out to Catherine. So pure. So noble.
So noble, yet so woebegone.
Though Frank and I may seem the picture of connubial
bliss . . .

CHEF

I am a breast without a nipple.
I am a watch-tower without a beacon.
I am the gall in an oak-apple.

MAMAH

I'm destined for ever to do crewelwork
on Goethe's high-and-mighty quatrains.

CHEF

I am the birch stripped of its bark.
I am a raven swooping over the squadron.
I am a hang-nail on a finger.
I am the eye that looks askance.

MAMAH

Compared to recent events in Morocco and
Montenegro,
all pales to insignificance.
The Vandals and Huns, the Goths under Alaric,
come sweeping back across the land
to build upon the built-up dark.
I hear them snort and snicker.

CHEF

I am a flint that holds no spark.
I am the rain falling at a slant.
I am a half-moon-shaped gold torc.
I am a sponge steeped in vinegar.

I am the hart. I am the hind.
I am the green and burning tree.
I am the cloud no bigger than a hand.
I will go down in history.

Orchestral Interlude

SCENE 3

14 August 1914. The Cliff Dwellers' Club, Chicago. Lights up on
SULLIVAN, *alone, stage right. He rises unsteadily, fingertips on*
table, to greet WRIGHT.

SULLIVAN

Frank.

WRIGHT

Lieber Meister.

(*They shake hands*.)

SULLIVAN

You're well, I trust.

WRIGHT

I'm well. And you?

SULLIVAN

So so.

WRIGHT

I often think of you perched on a ledge
at the Cliff Dwellers' Club
like an Anasazi
in Canyon De Chelly or Mesa Verde.

66

SULLIVAN

An Anasazi? You speak far better than you know.
The Anasazi were eclipsed
by the Hopi and the Navaho.

WRIGHT

The Hopi, the Haida, the Huron, the Hunkpapa Sioux
might have taught the Greeks and Romans
a lesson in harmony.

SULLIVAN

I know, I know, I know, I know, I know;
I know only too well why you see me 'perched on a

ledge'

of the Cliff Dwellers' Club:
I am Prometheus on his rock.
(SULLIVAN *raises his glass.*)
There's an eagle or vulture
feeding on my liver.
(*He drains the glass.*)
I know only too well why you see me hanging in chains,
full of self-pity, pie-eyed, peripheral.

WRIGHT

No, no, no, no, no;
when I see you perched on a ledge
at the Cliff Dwellers' Club
I'm thinking of your dream of an architecture –
to borrow your phrase – 'virile
and indigenous'.

SULLIVAN

Do you mean 'borrow' or 'purloin'?

WRIGHT

I mean 'borrow'.

SULLIVAN

It's a sore point, Frank.

WRIGHT

I know, I know, I know, I know, I know;
I'm thinking of your dream of a mile-high building
with a huge tap-root,
every inch a proud and soaring thing.

SULLIVAN

It's a sore point, Frank.

(*Pause.*)

What of your own dreams?

WRIGHT

I had a dream of a house that hill might marry.
Its walls are of stone from a local quarry.
Its roof bespeaks
the strength of native oak.
The hill is a mass of apple trees in bloom,
gooseberries, cherries, plums,
heavy horses and Holstein cows,
hens and ducks and swans and geese.

SULLIVAN

You're taking up agriculture?

WRIGHT

I had enough of that as a kid;
all pulling tits and shovelling shit.

SULLIVAN

You'll leave it, then, to the hired help?

WRIGHT

I know, I know, I know, I know, I know;
I know the virtue
of self-reliance.

But there's even greater virtue
in giving employment.

                    SULLIVAN
(*Calling out*)
      Another brandy and *crème de menthe*.

                    WRIGHT
Even now I'm consumed by guilt
at having to let someone go.

                    SULLIVAN
You want something?

                    WRIGHT
Nothing. I'm not much of a tippler.

                    SULLIVAN
I'm thinking more of the social purpose
of art and architecture.
It should be more than mere ornament.
It should do more than revel in itself
like a porpoise
turning on its own spit.

                    WRIGHT
It should be more than 'frozen music',
to borrow a phrase from Goethe.

                    SULLIVAN
A phrase Goethe purloined from Schelling.

                    WRIGHT
Do you mean 'purloined' or 'borrowed'?

                    SULLIVAN
I mean 'purloined'.

(*A* WAITER *enters, bearing a drink on a tray.*)

WAITER

Mr Sullivan, sir. Your brandy and *crème de menthe*.

(*The* WAITER *exits.*)

WRIGHT

This fellow I had to let go, my chef,
is a native of Barbados.
He used to work at the Cliff Dwellers' Club.

SULLIVAN

A paradox, Frank. How to achieve
a native architecture the natives might afford.

WRIGHT

There's Midway Gardens,
where 'earth and air and fire and water
are all somehow integral',
to borrow another phrase from Goethe.

SULLIVAN

A phrase Goethe purloined from Tobler.

WRIGHT

Do you mean 'purloined' or 'borrowed'?

SULLIVAN

I mean 'purloined'.

WRIGHT

There's still Midway Gardens;
there's art for the masses.

SULLIVAN

Please, Frank. You know I simply can't abide
your being glib;

I don't mean bread and circuses:
I don't mean a beer-garden.

WRIGHT

Be it beer-garden, byre, basilica, bank –
they should all be organic, don't you think?
Form follows function. Form and function are one.

SULLIVAN

A phrase you purloined, Frank, from me.

WRIGHT

Do you mean 'purloined' or 'borrowed'?

SULLIVAN

I mean 'purloined'.

(WRIGHT *moves towards the window*.)

WRIGHT

You were my *Lieber Meister*. I was 'a pencil in your
hand'.

SULLIVAN

It's a sore point, Frank.

WRIGHT

Together we would make our mark
on the clean slate of America.

SULLIVAN

But your ambition . . .

WRIGHT

Or your pride –

SULLIVAN

I think I know exactly which –

71

WRIGHT

Would drive a wedge
between us.

SULLIVAN

It's a sore point, Frank.

WRIGHT

(*Moving back towards* SULLIVAN.)
Is there no balm in Gilead?

(SULLIVAN *gets to his feet, again steadying himself on the table*.)

SULLIVAN

Would that there were, Frank; would that there were:
for ten long years I've cowered in the Gothic arch
of your Leviathan,
bowed under by the jawbone of a whale.
How you would damn
me with faint praise, then steal my thunder
as Prometheus stole fire,
all to the greater glory of your name;
there's malice in your magnanimity.

WRIGHT

(*Turning away*)
For ten long years I've tried to heal the breach
between myself and Louis Sullivan.
He knows only too well
how great I deem
him to be. He was my first mentor.
He was the first to fire
my imagination. I am the keeper of that flame;
why should he hold me in such enmity?

DUET

SULLIVAN: { For ten long years I've cowered in the Gothic arch
WRIGHT: { For ten long years I've tried to heal the breach

72

SULLIVAN: { of your Leviathan,
WRIGHT: { between myself and Louis Sullivan.

SULLIVAN: { bowed under by the jawbone of a whale.
WRIGHT: { He knows only too well

SULLIVAN: { How you would damn
WRIGHT: { how great I deem

SULLIVAN: { me with faint praise, then steal my thunder
WRIGHT: { him to be. He was my first mentor.

SULLIVAN: { as Prometheus stole fire,
WRIGHT: { He was the first to fire

SULLIVAN: { all to the greater glory of his name;
WRIGHT: { my imagination. I am the keeper of that flame;

SULLIVAN: { there's malice in your magnanimity.
WRIGHT: { why should he hold me in such enmity?

WRIGHT

Yet we hold so much in common.

SULLIVAN

So much?

WRIGHT

So much. The fact that we're both Celts.
I often think of you perched on a ledge
at the Cliff Dwellers' Club
like an Irish high king
on the ramparts of Tara.

SULLIVAN

Not Tara, Frank. The parapets of Troy.
The Irish are 'a pack of hounds
dragging down every noble stag'.

WRIGHT

Goethe?

SULLIVAN

Goethe.

(*The two remain motionless, as though reaching out to each other, yet unable to touch. An agitated* EDWIN CHENEY *rushes in.*)

WRIGHT

Eddie?
Why so crestfallen? So forlorn?

EDWIN

For three long hours I've tried to reach
you by telephone,
all to no avail.
(EDWIN *takes a telegram from his breast pocket.*)
I've had this telegram
from Spring Green. I can hardly bear its candour.

WRIGHT

Read it, man.

EDWIN

'TALIESIN DESTROYED BY FIRE.'

WRIGHT

By fire? And Mamah?

EDWIN

Nothing.

WRIGHT

Nothing?

EDWIN

Please, Frank. Try not to be distraught.

SULLIVAN

I'm sorry, Frank.

EDWIN

Quickly, now. We must be off.

WRIGHT

I know, I know, I know, I know, I know.

EDWIN

We can still catch the 5.05.

WRIGHT

The 5.05?

EDWIN

The train. It's almost five o'clock.

(EDWIN *has helped* WRIGHT *into his coat; he now steers him out.*
SULLIVAN *calls after them.*)

SULLIVAN

Please, Frank. Please don't go.

(SULLIVAN *goes over to the window.*)

I know, I know, I know, I know, I know;
for ten long years I've perched on a ledge
at the Cliff Dwellers' Club;
I've stood on the parapets of Troy
like Hector sighing for a sail.
Now I stand on the edge of an abyss.
I look into the chasm
between myself and Frank Lloyd Wright;
we can never be reconciled.

(SULLIVAN *moves back towards his table and chair.*)

So it is that the valley of disenchantment

(SULLIVAN *picks up his glass.*)

gives way to the Slough of Despond.

(SULLIVAN *is overcome by a fit of coughing; he sets the glass back on the table, takes out a handkerchief.*)

It's a sore point, Frank. It's a sore point.
There's a lump in my throat.
My mouth is full of bile.
I cry out from the Slough of Despond
while the Mohawk, the Shawnee, the Delaware,
under Thayendanegea, Tecumseh and Tammany
come sweeping back across the land
that was not 'borrowed' but 'purloined';

De profundis exclamavi ad Te Dominum.

SCENE 4

15 August 1914. The aftermath of the fire at Taliesin, the ruins of which are still smouldering. The 'Yellow Devil' is upstage, a little grubby but by and large unscathed; the canopy is down and the rear of the car contains the two plain caskets of the Cheney children. As in Act 1 Scene 2, the lighting will suggest a progress, this time from midnight to dawn. A CHORUS *of* FIREMEN, STAFF *and* TOWNSPEOPLE *are ranged about in attitudes of exhaustion and despair.*

CHORUS

(A cappella)

Out of the depths we heard them cry again,
out of the depths of hell;
we formed a human chain
to bring water from the well.

However deep the well,
it would all too soon run dry.
It was all to no avail;
we did little more than stand by.

Our efforts were all in vain;
we did little more than stand by
as bricks took wing and a black rain
fell from the sky.

For although the sky was bright,
bright as at Pentecost,
it was not until first light
that we could count the cost.

The door was shut. We broke it down.
We mounted the burning stair.
Then and only then
were we truly made aware.

(WRIGHT *and* EDWIN CHENEY *enter, their faces smeared with soot,
their sleeves rolled up and their coats over their arms.*)

Only then could we tell

WRIGHT

Emil Brodelle . . .

CHORUS

what havoc Carleton had wreaked.

Only then could we take toll
of his cruel, cruel work.

We laid them out to rest
on . . .

WRIGHT

Ernest Weston . . .

　　　. . . the muddy, muddy ground.

As if wild clove and mint
might somehow absolve the blame . . .

WRIGHT

David Lindblom.

CHORUS

Wright knelt by each sheeted mound
and heaped it with boughs and blooms.

As if sumach and sassafras
might somehow ease the rancour . . .

WRIGHT

Thomas Brunker . . .

CHORUS

As if cedar and sweet grass
might somehow cure the canker,

he covered each face
with sassafras and sumach
and vetches and violets.
Carleton, meanwhile, has vanished without trace;
our mouths are full of smoke.

WRIGHT

Has anybody been left out?

EDWIN

Please, Frank.

WRIGHT

For ten long hours they were trapped in the hump-
　　　　　　　　　　　　　　　backed whale
of this so-called 'prairie house':

the truth is that I myself am the whale;
I am both Ahab and Ishmael.

EDWIN

Please, Frank.

WRIGHT

The truth is that my mouth is full of steel;
so much so, that I've been flayed and flensed
and my blubber rendered
to the cauldron of boiling oil
that poured down on Mamah and your children.

EDWIN

Please, Frank. Please don't fan the embers.

WRIGHT

Forgive me, Ed.
It's cost us both. It's cost us both the earth.
My mouth is full of mud.

EDWIN

It sounds as if you might believe in fate.

WRIGHT

It seems somehow appropriate
that a fire should crack the boulder
in the prairie of my heart;
my mouth is full of stones.

EDWIN

I used to believe that some Master Builder
assigned Sullivan his rock
and you your boulder

(EDWIN *removes a flint from his pocket and hands it to* WRIGHT.)

and me this little pot-sherd.

79

WRIGHT

(*Examining it*)

She pierced my heart like an arrowhead.

EDWIN

It's no arrowhead, Frank. It's a broken-off flint.
Accept it as a token
of the randomness of things.

WRIGHT

The *seeming* randomness of things.

EDWIN

The sheer randomness of things.
This broken-off flint
is an emblem of the haphazard;
it's no more part of some grand design
than Carleton taking a violent
turn and setting fire to Taliesin.

WRIGHT

No, no, no, no, no;
had I not set myself above the 'average' laws
for 'average' men,
this might still be our Avalon,
our Chapel of the Holy Grail.

EDWIN

The Holy Grail's a stove-in pail.
The Holy Rood's a splintered tree.
I view your notion of destiny
with nothing less than disdain.
That there is some grand design
is the height of self-delusion.

WRIGHT

Is there no balm in Gilead?

EDWIN

Would that there were, Frank; would that there were.

WRIGHT

Is there no holy chrism
with which to anoint her brow?

EDWIN

Her brow is ashen, Frank. Her hand is cold.
(*Pause.*)
I'm going now.

WRIGHT

Please don't go.

(EDWIN *gets into the 'Yellow Devil'*.)

EDWIN

I must go. I must attend to the burial
of my children.

WRIGHT

And Mamah?

EDWIN

Would that I could, Frank. Would that I could.

WRIGHT

Goodbye, Ed.

EDWIN

My mouth is full of wormwood. My mouth is full of
aloes.

(EDWIN *slowly drives off. Part of the* CHORUS *falls in behind the*
'Yellow Devil' to form an impromptu cortège.)

Out of the depths we heard them cry again;
out of the depths of hell.
For ten long hours they hung in chains.
They were stretched on the burning wheel.

They were stretched on the burning wheel.
We heard them weep and gnash
their teeth. We heard them weep and wail.
Our mouths are full of ash.

For ten long hours we heard them scream
out in their torture.
Is their suffering part of a grand scheme?
Is there some hidden order?

WRIGHT

I stand on the edge of an abyss.
I look into a chasm.

(WRIGHT, *who has moved upstage, ponders the flint*.)

So much for my so-called 'lack of scruples'.
So much for my 'ostracism'.

(WRIGHT *puts the flint in his pocket*.)

She pierced my heart like an arrowhead.
And her scent? Was it musk?
Not musk. Cedar perhaps. Perhaps night-scented stock.
Not stock. Sassafras.
Not sassafras. Maple.
Not maple. Pine;
the scent of a plain pine box
where she'll lie in this hallowed ground.
Would that she might take me in her arms.
Would that I might fill the grave myself.

(*The* MAID *rushes in, not noticing* WRIGHT'*s presence*.)

He's found. We've found the chef.

Who? How? What? Where? When?

For twenty long hours we hunted high and low
for Carleton. Little did we know

that he was all the while hiding in the maze
of Taliesin. We found him under a mass

of rubble in the furnace room.
The truth is that we heard his muffled screams

out of the depths of Taliesin.
His body was a mass of lesions

and lacerations, welts and weals;
It looked as if this embodiment of evil

had been hit on the head with a shovel.
He lay in the maw of a hump-backed whale

like a lump of ambergris.
I began to cry in rhythm with his cries

that were less cries than gasps or gurgles:
the wretch had swallowed hydrochloric

acid; his throat was a ghastly hole.
I could easily make out the lump of gristle

and keratin that was his Adam's apple.
I myself am scarcely able

to speak, much less atone
for my anger. My mouth is full of iodine.

(*The* MAID *has unsuspectingly backed into* WRIGHT, *who drops his coat in the confusion.*)

WRIGHT

Miriam.

(*The* MAID *picks up the coat, from the breast pocket of which has fallen a tattered piece of paper, which she hands to* WRIGHT.)

MAID

Not Miriam. Mabel.

(*The* MAID *joins the* CHORUS *while* WRIGHT *unfolds the piece of paper.*)

WRIGHT

Not maple. Pine;
the scent of a plain pine box
where she'll lie in this hallowed ground.

(WRIGHT *reads from the Goethe translation.*)

She sweeps us off our feet
and dances round and round,
then flings us back, exhausted,
on the muddy ground.

(*The disembodied voice of* MAMAH CHENEY *now ghosts* WRIGHT.)

WRIGHT AND MAMAH

We lie on the muddy ground
and take her in our arms.
She's nowhere to be found
amongst her thousand forms.

WRIGHT, MAMAH AND CHORUS

Though she takes a thousand forms
she's always in one place.

She takes us in her arms.
She holds us in a fast embrace.

Would that she might take me in her arms.
Would that I might fill the grave myself.

That something is destroyed
is itself a grand illusion.

(MAMAH *and the* CHORUS *drop out as* WRIGHT *continues alone,*
stage right, in the area we associate with SULLIVAN.)

I will make of their *De Profundis*
a *Kyrie Eleison*.
I think of the balsam-fir
that springs up a hundredfold
in the aftermath of a forest fire;
surely there is balm in Gilead?
The Gila Apache, the Adirondack,
the mighty Assiniboine,
all perceived the intricate
order in even a pine cone.
That Mamah's dead and gone
is itself a grand illusion;
she'll be both key- and corner-stone
of a newly built Taliesin.
She is the house. She is the hill.
She is the house that hill might marry.
I will dedicate both field and hall
to Mamah's memory.
She is within us all,
we are all within Nature.
Through winter and summer, spring and fall,
we will – we must – endure.
Would that the Osage, bows in hand,

the Ostrogoths under Theodoric,
might come sweeping back across the land . . .
It all goes back to those cowboy books
my mama gave me as a child.
I will fill her plain pine box
with wild
flowers and marjoram
and mulberry leaves.
Would that she might take me in her arms.
Would that I myself
might fill her unmarked grave.
Why mark the spot where desolation began
and ended? It followed the curve
of an old toboggan.
So much, then, for the domain
of the Ottawa, the Ojibwa, the Omaha Sioux,
the Potawottoman;
so much for all that tittle-tattle:
they have all gone into the built-up dark.
Yet my heart goes out to Louis Sullivan.
In the prairie of my heart, a little
bird cries out against oblivion;
I know, I know, I know, I know, I know.
A shrike, perhaps. A siskin, or some such finch.
So much. So much. So much . . . So . . .